Scriptural Rosary for Children

REV. JUDE WINKLER, OFM Conv.

Imprimi Potest: Michael Kolodziej, OFM Conv., Minister Provincial of St. Anthony of Padua Province (USA)
Nihil Obstat: Rev. James M. Cafone, M.A., S.T.D., Censor Librorum
Imprimatur: ✠ **Most Rev. John J. Myers, J.C.D., D.D.**, Archbishop of Newark

The Nihil Obstat and Imprimatur are official declarations that a book or pamphlet is free of doctrinal or moral error. No implication is contained therein that those who have granted the Nihil Obstat and Imprimatur agree with the contents, opinions or statements expressed.

> ## *"Whatever you ask through the Rosary shall be granted."*
>
> Promise of Our Lady to St. Dominic

How the Rosary Began

There are a number of different stories about how the Holy Rosary began. Two of the oldest stories tell us why people needed the Rosary and who helped spread its use throughout the world.

In the early days of the Church, people wanted to make their daily lives more holy. When they would ask spiritual leaders how they could do this, the leaders would tell them that they should meditate on the Mysteries of God's love. They asked these spiritual guides how long they should meditate on these Mysteries (for they had no clocks or watches). The answer was that they should meditate for as long as it would take to pray one Our Father and ten Hail Marys.

Even if this is how the Rosary began, it was St. Dominic, the founder of the Dominicans, who spread the practice of praying it every day. He preached at the beginning of the thirteenth century, a time when many people had turned away from God. Dominic devoted himself to preaching the Word of God to those who had lost their Faith.

There is a legend that the Blessed Virgin Mary appeared to St. Dominic and gave him a Rosary, telling him to pray it so that sinners would be converted.

Lourdes and Fatima

There have been a number of signs and appear-
ances throughout the ages that show us the
importance of the Rosary.

When the Blessed Virgin Mary appeared in
Lourdes, France, in 1858, St. Bernadette prayed
the Rosary with her. After they had finished praying it, Mary revealed to Bernadette that she was
"the Immaculate Conception." Bernadette did not
even understand what this meant for this truth of
the Faith had only just been declared. It means

that Mary was protected from the damage of sin from the moment of her conception.

Then, in 1917, the Blessed Virgin Mary appeared to three young children in Fatima, Portugal. This was a very difficult time in the world. World War I was tearing apart nations. The Communists, who deny that God exists, were about to take power in Russia.

Mary told the children that they should pray the Rosary. She called it a powerful weapon against selfishness and sin. This message is just as true today as it was when Mary appeared at Lourdes and Fatima.

How to Pray the Rosary

One can pray the Rosary with a group of people or alone. One can pray this devotion in church, at home, or anywhere.

We begin the Rosary with the Sign of the Cross (for this is the way that we begin all of our prayers).

After this, we pray the Apostles' Creed. This is a very ancient prayer that proclaims the important truths of our Faith.

After the Apostles' Creed, we pray one Our Father, three Hail Marys, and one Glory be.

We now come to the most important reason why we pray the Rosary: to meditate on the Mysteries of our Faith. We proclaim each of the five Mysteries, followed by one Our Father, ten Hail Marys, and one Glory be.

Remember, the reason for praying the Rosary is not to tally how many prayers we can say. It is to meditate on God's love as shown in the lives of Jesus and Mary. This is why we hold the Rosary while we pray, so that we can keep track of the number of prayers we have said without having to count them.

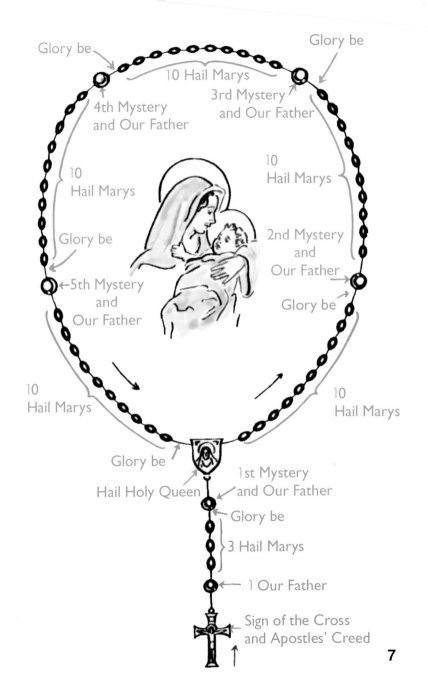

Glory be

Glory be

10 Hail Marys

3rd Mystery
and Our Father

4th Mystery
and Our Father

10
Hail Marys

10
Hail Marys

Glory be

2nd Mystery
and
Our Father

←5th Mystery
and
Our Father

Glory be

10
Hail Marys

10
Hail Marys

Glory be

1st Mystery
and Our Father

Hail Holy Queen

Glory be

3 Hail Marys

1 Our Father

Sign of the Cross
and Apostles' Creed

7

The Joyful Mysteries

These are the Mysteries that we pray on Mondays and Saturdays, the Sundays of Advent, and Sundays from Epiphany until Lent:

1. The Annunciation

2. The Visitation

3. The Birth of Jesus

4. The Presentation of Jesus in the Temple

5. The Finding of Jesus in the Temple

To help us meditate upon them, we will read some verses from the Bible that tell us what happened. If there is no such passage from Scripture, we will read some thoughts that help us reflect on the Mystery.

The First Joyful Mystery: The Annunciation

Luke 1:26-28, 30-31, 38

In the sixth month, the Angel Gabriel was sent by God to a town in Galilee called Nazareth, to a Virgin betrothed to a man named Joseph, of the house of David. The Virgin's name was Mary.

The Angel came to her and said, "Hail, full of grace! The Lord is with you." The Angel also said, "Do not be afraid, Mary, for you have found favor with God. Behold, you will conceive in your womb and bear a Son, and you will name Him Jesus." Mary said, "Behold, I am the servant of the Lord. Let it be done to me according to your word."

9

The Second Joyful Mystery: The Visitation

Luke 1:39-43

Mary set out and journeyed in haste to a town of Judah where she entered the house of Zechariah and greeted Elizabeth, her cousin who was with child. When Elizabeth heard Mary's greeting, the baby leaped in her womb.

Then Elizabeth exclaimed with a loud cry, "Blessed are you among women, and blessed is the Fruit of your womb. And why am I so greatly favored that the Mother of my Lord should visit me?"

The Third Joyful Mystery: The Birth of Jesus

Luke 2:1, 4, 6-7

In those days, a decree was issued by Caesar Augustus that a census should be taken throughout the entire world. Joseph therefore went from the town of Nazareth in Galilee to Judea, to the city of David called Bethlehem, because he was of the house and family of David.

While Joseph and Mary were there, the time came for her to have her Child. She wrapped Him in swaddling clothes and laid Him in a manger, because there was no room for them in the inn.

The Fourth Joyful Mystery:
The Presentation of Jesus in the Temple

Luke 2:22, 27-30, 38

When the days for their purification were completed according to the Law of Moses, they brought the Child up to Jerusalem to present Him to the Lord.

Prompted by the Spirit, Simeon came into the Temple. He took Jesus in his arms and praised God, saying, "Now, Lord, You may dismiss Your servant in peace, for my eyes have seen Your salvation."

At that moment, Anna came forward and began to praise God, while she spoke about the Child.

The Fifth Joyful Mystery:
The Finding of Jesus in the Temple

Luke 2:42-43, 46, 49

When Jesus was twelve years old, the Holy Family made the journey for the feast of Passover. When the days of the feast were over and they set off for home, the Boy Jesus stayed behind in Jerusalem.

After three days Mary and Joseph found Him in the Temple, where He was sitting among the teachers, listening to them and asking them questions.

Jesus said to Mary and Joseph, "Why were you searching for Me? Did you not know that I must be in My Father's house?"

13

The Luminous Mysteries

These are the Mysteries that we pray on Thursdays:

1. The Baptism of Jesus
2. The Wedding Feast at Cana
3. The Proclamation of the Kingdom of God
4. The Transfiguration
5. The Institution of the Eucharist

To help us meditate upon them, we will read some verses from the Bible that tell us what happened. If there is no such passage from Scripture, we will read some thoughts that help us reflect on the Mystery.

The First Luminous Mystery: The Baptism of Jesus

Matthew 3:13-15, 16-17

Jesus arrived from Galilee and came to John at the Jordan to be baptized by him. John tried to dissuade Him, saying, "Why do You come to me? I am the one who needs to be baptized by You." But Jesus said to him in reply, "For the present, let it be thus."

After Jesus had been baptized, as He came up from the water, suddenly the heavens were opened and He beheld the Spirit of God descending like a dove and alighting on Him. And a voice came from heaven, saying, "This is My beloved Son, in Whom I am well pleased."

The Second Luminous Mystery:
The Wedding Feast at Cana

John 2:3, 6-7, 8-9, 11

When the wine was exhausted at a wedding, the Mother of Jesus said to Him, "They have no wine." Now standing nearby there were six stone water jars, each holding twenty to thirty gallons. Jesus instructed the servants, "Fill the jars with water."

The servants brought some of the water to the steward. The steward tasted the water that had become wine. Jesus performed this, the first of His signs, at Cana in Galilee.

The Third Luminous Mystery:
The Proclamation of the Kingdom of God

Matthew 13:31-32, 45-46

The kingdom of God is like a mustard seed that a man took and sowed in his field. It is the smallest of all the seeds, but when it has grown it is the greatest of plants and becomes a tree large enough for the birds to come and make nests in its branches.

The kingdom of God is like a merchant searching for fine pearls. When he found one of great value, he went off and sold everything he had and bought it.

The Fourth Luminous Mystery:
The Transfiguration

Matthew 17:1-3, 5

Jesus took Peter and James and his brother John and led them up a high mountain by themselves. And in their presence He was transfigured; His face shone like the sun, and His clothes became dazzling white. Then Moses and Elijah appeared to them, conversing with Him.

Then a cloud came and cast its shadow over them. A voice came out of the cloud, saying, "This is My Son, My Chosen One. Listen to Him."

The Fifth Luminous Mystery:
The Institution of the Eucharist

Matthew 26:26; Luke 22:19; Matthew 26:27-28

While they were eating, Jesus took bread, and after He had pronounced the blessing, He broke it and gave it to His disciples, saying, "Take this and eat; this is My Body, which will be given for you. Do this in memory of Me."

Then He took a cup, and after offering thanks, He gave it to them, saying, "Drink from this, all of you. For this is My Blood of the covenant, which will be shed on behalf of many for the forgiveness of sins."

The Sorrowful Mysteries

These are the Mysteries that we pray on Tuesdays and Fridays throughout the year, and daily from Ash Wednesday until Easter Sunday:

1. The Agony in the Garden
2. The Scourging at the Pillar
3. The Crowning with Thorns
4. Jesus Carries His Cross
5. Jesus Dies on the Cross

To help us meditate upon them, we will read some verses from the Bible that tell us what happened. If there is no such passage from Scripture, we will read some thoughts that help us reflect on the Mystery.

The First Sorrowful Mystery:
The Agony in the Garden

Mark 14:32-33, 35-36; Luke 22:43

Jesus and the disciples went to a place that was called Gethsemane, and Jesus said to His disciples, "Sit here while I pray." He took with Him Peter and James and John, and He began to suffer distress.

Moving on a little farther, He threw himself on the ground and prayed that, if it were possible, the hour might pass Him by, saying, "Abba, Father, for You all things are possible. Take this cup from Me. Yet not My will but Yours be done." Then an Angel from heaven appeared to Him and gave Him strength.

The Second Sorrowful Mystery:
The Scourging at the Pillar

Matthew 27:24-26; 1 Peter 2:23

When Pilate saw that a riot was about to occur, he took some water and washed his hands in full view of the crowd, saying, "I am innocent of this Man's Blood." He then released Barabbas to them, and had Jesus scourged.

When Jesus was abused, He did not retaliate. When He suffered, He made no threats, but He placed His trust in the One Who judges justly.

The Third Sorrowful Mystery:
The Crowning with Thorns

Matthew 27:27-30

The governor's soldiers took Jesus inside the prae-torium and gathered the whole cohort around Him. They stripped Him and put a scarlet robe on Him, and after twisting some thorns into a crown, they placed it on His head and put a reed in His right hand.

Bending the knee before Him, they mocked Him, saying, "Hail, King of the Jews!" The soldiers spat upon Jesus, and taking a reed, used it to strike Him on the head.

The Fourth Sorrowful Mystery:
Jesus Carries His Cross

Luke 23:26-27, 32

As they led Jesus away, they seized a man from Cyrene named Simon, who was returning from the country. They put the Cross on his back and forced him to carry it behind Jesus. A large number of people followed Jesus, among them many women who were mourning and lamenting over Him.

There were also two others, both criminals, who were led away to be executed with Him.

The Fifth Sorrowful Mystery:
Jesus Dies on the Cross

Mark 15:25, 29, 33-34, 37

It was around nine o'clock in the morning when they crucified Him. Those people who passed by jeered at Him, shaking their heads.

Beginning at midday, there was darkness over the whole land until three in the afternoon. At three o'clock, Jesus cried out in a loud voice, "My God, My God, why have You forsaken Me?" Then Jesus cried out in a loud voice and breathed His last.

The Glorious Mysteries

These are the Mysteries that we pray on Wednesdays and Sundays from Easter until Advent:

1. The Resurrection
2. The Ascension
3. The Descent of the Holy Spirit
4. The Assumption
5. The Crowning of the Blessed Virgin Mary

To help us meditate upon them, we will read some verses from the Bible that tell us what happened. If there is no such passage from Scripture, we will read some thoughts that help us reflect on the Mystery.

The First Glorious Mystery: The Resurrection

Luke 24:1-6

At daybreak on the first day of the week, the women came to the tomb with spices they had prepared. They found the stone rolled away from the tomb, but when they went inside, they did not find the Body of the Lord Jesus.

Suddenly two men in dazzling clothes appeared at their side. They said to the women, "Why do you look among the dead for One Who is alive? Jesus is not here. He has been raised."

The Second Glorious Mystery:
The Ascension

Acts 1:9-11

Jesus was lifted up as the disciples looked on, and a cloud took Him from their sight.

While He was departing as they gazed upward toward the sky, suddenly two men dressed in white robes stood beside them, and they said, "Men of Galilee, why are you standing there looking up into the sky? This Jesus Who has been taken from you into heaven will come back in the same way you have seen Him going into heaven."

The Third Glorious Mystery:
The Descent of the Holy Spirit

Acts 2:1-4

When the day of Pentecost arrived, they were all assembled together in one place. Suddenly, there came from heaven a sound similar to that of a violent wind, and it filled the entire house in which they were sitting.

There appeared tongues of fire, which separated and came to rest on each one of them. All of them were filled with the Holy Spirit, and they began to speak in different languages, as the Spirit enabled them to do.

The Fourth Glorious Mystery: The Assumption

Luke 1:46-54

Mary said, "My soul proclaims the greatness of the Lord, and my spirit rejoices in God my Savior. For He has looked with favor on the lowliness of His servant; henceforth, all generations will call me blessed.

"The Mighty One has done great things for me, and holy is His Name. His mercy is shown from age to age to those who fear Him. . . . He has come to the aid of Israel His servant, ever mindful of His merciful love."

The Fifth Glorious Mystery:
The Crowning of the Blessed Virgin Mary

Romans 8:14-15, 17, 30

Those who are led by the Spirit of God are children of God. You did not receive a spirit of slavery leading to fear; rather, you received the Spirit of adoption. . . . If we are children of God, then we are heirs—heirs of God and joint heirs with Christ.

Those whom He predestined He also called, and those whom He called He also justified, and those whom He justified He also glorified.

After one has prayed all five decades of the Rosary, one can say the following prayer.

O God, whose only-begotten Son, by His life, death and resurrection, has purchased for us the rewards of eternal life; grant, we ask You, that, meditating upon these Mysteries of the Most Holy Rosary of the Blessed Virgin Mary, we may imitate what they contain and obtain what they promise, through the same Christ our Lord. Amen.

We then close our recitation of the Rosary with the Sign of the Cross.